HARMONY *over* HUSTLE

EMPOWERING **I AM STATEMENTS** COLORING BOOK

By Hala Dabboussy

This book belongs to

INSTRUCTIONS

- Every page has an *I AM Statement* and a mandala design that you can color

- Use bright coloring pencils or pens to express your creativity

- To create an even more powerful *I AM Statement*, complete that sentence by answering BECAUSE or SO THAT

- Pull out the colored page

- Hang it as a visual reminder of your awesomeness

- The last pages are for you to add your own *I AM Statements*

A MESSAGE FROM THE AUTHOR

I would like to share with you the
I AM Statement that saved my life:

I AM A POWERHOUSE,
(BECAUSE/ SO THAT)
I CAN HANDLE ANYTHING
LIFE THROWS AT ME.

In 2022 I suffered from a ruptured brain aneurysm.
I almost died.

Because this was my go-to *I AM Statement* for a couple of years, when I was admitted in ICU, a dear friend printed the above *I AM Statement* and hung it on the wall opposite my ICU bed. I used to read it every day! and I believed it! EVERYDAY!

What I would love for you to do is to finish the *I AM Statements* inside the book by answering *BECAUSE* or *SO THAT* and use it as a daily visual reminder to overcome any bump in your road to live a harmonious life.

Embrace the Power of
Harmony over Hustle!

I AM
AUTHENTIC

I AM HAPPY

I AM
CREATIVE

I AM
SMART

I AM
BLESSED

I AM
INTENTIONAL

I AM
CONFIDENT

I AM
HELPFUL

I AM
KIND

I AM
WORTHY

I AM
UNIQUE

I AM
SPECIAL

I AM
LOVED

I AM STRONG

I AM
CONTENT

I AM
DRIVEN

I AM
TALENTED

I AM
HAPPY

I AM
FOCUSED

I AM
HEALTHY

I AM
WEALTHY

I AM PROUD

I AM
POSITIVE

I AM
PURPOSEFUL

I AM
CARING

I AM A LEADER

I AM A POWERHOUSE

I AM
LOVING

I AM
SPIRITUAL

I AM
HOPEFUL

I AM
GENEROUS

I AM
FAIR

I AM ROOTED

I AM AWESOME

I AM
CURIOUS

I AM
HUMBLE

I AM
CAPABLE

I AM
BEAUTIFUL

I AM
FREE

I AM
GENUINE

I AM
CONNECTED

I AM
INSPIRED

I AM
SINCERE

I AM EMPOWERED

I AM
PRESENT

I AM

I AM

Made in the USA
Middletown, DE
15 May 2024

54340889R00057